Eternal Manifestations

80 Stories from the Life of ʿAllāma Tabātabāʾī

Compiled by Ahmad Luqmani

Copyright

Copyright © 2022 al-Burāq Publications.
All rights reserved. No part of this publication may be reproduced, distributed, or transmitted in any form or by any means, including photocopying, recording, or other electronic or mechanical methods, without the prior written permission of the publisher, except in the case of brief quotations embodied in critical reviews and certain other noncommercial uses permitted by copyright law. For permission requests, write to the publisher, addressed "Attention: Permissions [Eternal Manifestations: 80 Stories from the Life of ʿAllāma Tabātabāʾī]," at the email address below.

ISBN: 978-1-956276-09-1.
Printed and published by al-Burāq Publications.

Ordering Information
We offer discounts and promotions for wholesale purchases and for non-profit organizations, libraries, and other educational institutions. Contact us at the email below for further information.

www.al-Buraq.org
publications@al-Buraq.org

First Edition | May 2020
Second Edition | January 2022

Dedication

The publication of this book was made possible through the generous support of our donors.

Please recite *Sūrah al-Fātiha* and ask Allāh for the Divine reward (*thawāb*) to be conferred upon the donors and the souls of all those in whose memory their loved ones have contributed graciously towards the publication of *Eternal Manifestations: 80 Stories from the Life of 'Allāma Tabātabā'ī*.

Duaa al-Hujja

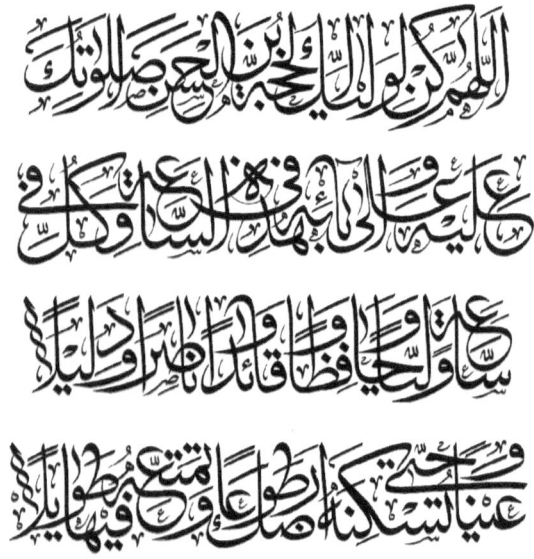

O Allah, be, for Your representative, the Hujjat (proof), son of al-Hasan, Your blessings be upon him and his forefathers, in this hour and in every hour: a guardian, a protector, a leader, a helper, a proof, and an eye until You make him live on the Earth, in obedience (to You), and cause him to live in it for a long time.

Table of Contents

Love for the Ahlul-Bayt (as) 1
    Ayatullah Ibrāhim Amīnī 1
    Hujjatulislām Doctor Ahmadī 2
    Shahīd Mutahharī 3
    Ayatullah Misbāh Yazdī 3
    'Allāma Tehrānī 4

Akhlāq (Manner / Character) 5
    Ayatullah Ibrāhīm Amīnī 5
    Ayatullah Jawādī Āmulī 6
    Ayatullah Ibrāhīm Amīnī 7
    'Allāma's daughter, Najma As-Sādāt Tabātabā'ī 7
    'Allāma's daughter 8

Akhlāq (Manner / Character) at Home 9
    'Allāma's daughter 9
    'Allāma's daughter 9
    'Allāma's daughter 10

At Home with his Wife 11
    Ayatullah Ibrāhīm Amīnī 11
    'Allāma's daughter 12
    Narrated by 'Allāma Tabātabā'ī 13

At Home with his Children 15
    'Allāma's daughter 15
    'Allāma's daughter 15
    'Allāma's daughter 16

'Allāma's daughter	16
'Allāma's daughter	17

Sincerity and Humility 18

Ayatullah Ja'far Subhānī	18
Hujjat ul-Islam Mūsawī Hamadānī	18
One of the Scholars of Qum	18
'Allāma Husayni Tehrānī	18
'Allāma Tehrānī	19
'Allāma Tehrānī	21
Ayatullah Ibrāhīm Amīnī	22
Ayatullah Misbāh Yazdī	23
'Allāma Tabātabā'ī's son-in-law	23
Ayatullah Jawādī Āmulī	24

Spirituality 26

Ayatullah Ibrāhīm Amīnī	26
'Allāma's daughter	26
Ayatullah Jawādī Āmulī	27
Shahīd Mutahharī	28

Allāma & the Qur'ān 29

Ayatullah Hasanzādeh Āmulī	29
'Allāma Tehrānī	29
Hujjatul Islam Mūsawī Hamadānī	30
'Allāma's daughter	30

Knowledge 31

Ayatullah Misbāh Yazdī	31
Shahid Mutahharī	32
'Allāma Sayyid Muhammad Husayn Tehrānī	33

Ayatullah Jawādī Āmulī..36
Ayatullah Jawādī Āmulī..36
Ayatullah Jawādī Āmulī..37
'Allāma's daughter..38
Narrated by 'Allāma Tabātabā'ī.............................38
'Allāma Tehrānī...39

Allāma as a Student 41
Narrated by 'Allāma Tabātabā'ī.............................41
Narrated by 'Allāma Tabātabā'ī.............................42
Narrated by 'Allāma Tabātabā'ī.............................44
Friend of 'Allāma Tabātabā'ī..................................45
As a Student of Ayatullah Qādhī..........................45
As a Student of Ayatullah Qādhī..........................47

Allāma as a Teacher 50
Ustād Rezā Ustādī 50
'Allāma Tehrānī...50
'Allāma Tehrānī...51

Academic Activities 55
Ayatullah Ibrāhīm Amīnī...55
Impact on the Hawza of Qum 55
Ayatullah Jawādī Āmulī..56
Ustād Ridhā Ustādī 57

Al-Mizan..58
Narrated by 'Allāma Tabātabā'ī.............................58
Narrated by 'Allāma Tabātabā'ī.............................58
Shahīd Mutahharī 59
Ayatullah Hasanzādeh Āmulī 60

Imām Mūsa Sadr narrated from Shaykh Muhammad Jawād Mughniye 60

Ayatullah Hasanzādeh Āmulī 60

Ayatullah Makārim Shīrāzī 61

'Allāma Sayyid Muhammad Husayn Tehrānī 62

Perseverance and Hard Work 64

Ayatullah Ja'far Subhānī 64

'Allāma's daughter 65

Spiritual Disclosures (Mukāshafāt) 67

Ayatullah Hasanzādeh Āmulī 67

Newspaper Jumhuriye Islāmi 67

Narrated by 'Allāma Tabātabā'ī 68

Narrated by 'Allāma Tabātabā'ī 68

Narrated by 'Allāma Tabātabā'ī 70

Last Days 73

Ayatullah Ibrāhīm Amini 73

Ayatullah Ibrāhīm Amīnī 74

One of the Scholars of Qum 75

Ayatullah Ibrāhīm Amīnī 76

Love for the Ahlul-Bayt (as)

Ayatullah Ibrāhim Amīnī

'Allāma Tabātabā'ī used to visit the shrine of Hazrat Ma'sūma (s) at least once every week. He would walk [to the shrine], and along the way, if he saw a discarded orange, cucumber or banana peel, he would use his staff to remove it from the sidewalk. During the summer he used to visit the holy city of Mashhad. When visiting the shrine of Imām Ridha (a) at night, he would sit in the area adjacent to the side of the shrine (*dharīh*) where Imām's head is buried. In a state of humbleness and humility he would then recite the *ziyārat* (greetings to the Imām). Whilst in Mashhad he would participate in the Maghrib and 'Ishā congregational prayers led by Ayatullah Sayyid Muhammad Hādi Mīlānī, sitting in a corner amongst the people [during the namaz].

'Allāma had an intimate relationship with the Prophet (s) and the Imāms (a). He would mention their names with extreme decorum and reverence, participate in gatherings where their deaths were mourned, and weep profusely for the tragedies that the Ahlul Bayt had faced.

Hujjatulislām Doctor Ahmadī

Marhūm 'Allāma's connection with the Ahlul-Bayt was one of complete love. Not once do I remember him mentioning the names of any one of the Imāmswithout respect. Each time he would enter the shrine of Imām Ridhā (a) in the holy city of Mashhad, I would see him place his trembling hands on the threshold and kiss it – his entire body quivering from the depths of his soul.

Occasionally in his presence we would ask him to pray for us. He would reply, *"Go and ask from Hazrat [Imām]. We have no special position here, everything is available from him."*

When he kissed the wooden frame of the shrine (*dharīh*), his entire being reflected a profound etiquette towards Imām Ridhā (a). With complete propriety (*adab*) and extreme love he would then recite his prayers in a corner. From the time he would enter until the time he left he conducted himself with *adab*.

Shahīd Mutahharī

A scholar once asked Shahīd Ayatullah Mutahharī, "Why do you respect 'Allāma Tabātabā'ī so much and say *may I be sacrificed for him?*"

He replied, I have seen many philosophers and mystics. My unique respect for 'Allāma is not related to his being a philosopher. Rather, my reverence stems from the fact that he is an enamored lover of the Ahlul-Bayt. [For example] 'Allāma Tabātabā'ī used to break his fast in the month of Ramadhān by kissing the shrine (*dharīh*) of Hazrat Ma'sūmā (a). He would walk to the holy shrine, kiss the *dharīh*, and then return to his home to eat. It is this characteristic of his that has captivated me to such a degree.

Ayatullah Misbāh Yazdī

Daily activities that occupied 'Allāma day and night did not prevent him from seeking intercession and exhibiting propriety (*adab*) for the AhlulBayt. Rather he recognized that he was indebted to their intercession for his situation. His respect for the words of the Ma'sūmīn was so great that even when dealing with traditions whose chains of narration were weak, he acted in a cautionary manner because of the possibility that they might be from the Ahlul-Bayt. In addition, he believed that even the slightest disrespect or ill-thought towards this pure family should not be tolerated.

'Allāma Tehrānī

Whenever the name of one of the Ma'sūmīn was mentioned, humility and etiquette would be apparent on 'Allāma's face. He had particular reverence for Imām Zamān [the 12th Holy Imam] – may we be sacrificed for him. He considered the position of the Prophet, Imāms and Hadhrat Siddāqa Kubrā [Sayyida Fatima] (a) to be beyond description. He had a humble, reverential and pious manner in respect to them, considered their position and status to be celestial, and had an in-depth knowledge of their actions and history.

Akhlāq (Manner / Character)

Ayatullah Ibrāhīm Amīnī

'Allāma was refined, kind, chaste, humble, sincere, lacking desire, patient, sweet and a great companion. For 30 years I was with 'Allāma, attending his classes, participating in his private Thursday night and Friday sessions, and benefiting from his presence as much as I could. Not once during this time do I remember him ever becoming angry or yelling at one of his students or speaking harshly or insulting anyone.

He used to teach his classes calmly and quietly, never raising his voice. He became familiar and made friends with others very quickly. He was so friendly with everyone, even a new student, that one might have thought they were two dear friends. He listened to everyone and always displayed signs of love and friendship. He was incredibly humble...and did not give importance to the number of his students, sometimes agreeing to teach only two or three individuals.

In private sessions he would normally remain quiet and calm. If he was asked a question, he would answer, and if not, he would maintain his silence. Occasionally if someone would refer to him as a Professor (*Ustād*), he would say, *"I do not like this title. We have gathered here as colleagues in thought so that we might discover the truths of Islam."*

'Allāma was very well mannered, listening to every individual and never interrupting anyone. If he heard the truth he would acknowledge it. He would avoid argumentative discussions, but willingly answer any sincere questions asked of him.

Ayatullah Jawādī Āmulī

'Allāma Tabātabā'ī's manner was one that conformed completely to the Qur'ān. Perhaps it can be said that his behavior had become the Qur'ān. Every verse that God has placed in the Qur'ān describing a perfect human being (*Insāne Kāmil*), we found it in 'Allāma's behavior to the extent that it is possible to be seen in an individual. His gatherings were those of perfect Islāmic etiquette and Godly character. It was rare for him to commit even an action which, without being a sin, was not the best course of action to take (*tarke ūla*). He never mentioned someone's name with ill-feeling, nor anyone's bad characteristics, and tried to always pray for the well-being of others.

Ayatullah Ibrāhīm Amīnī

ʻAllāma Tabātabā'ī was extremely kind and sentimental. He never forgot his friends and always kept in touch with them. He acted benevolently with his private students, and was attached to and familiar with them, and inquired about the situation of those who had moved to other cities.

ʻAllāma's daughter, Najma As-Sādāt Tabātabā'ī

One of the outstanding characteristics of my father was his close relationship with his students – especially Āghā Mutahharī. He himself used to say: every time I sit with my friends, it is as if the entire world lights up in my view. Truly I take pleasure [from their company].

'Allāma's daughter

'Allāma used to speak very little, and he also used to advise others to speak less. He regarded speaking a lot as a sign of a weak intellect. He talked very simply and in such a manner that sometimes people used to believe he was a regular individual, and not a scholar and a philosopher.

Akhlāq (Manner / Character) at Home

'Allāma's daughter

His manner and behavior at home was truly like that of Prophet Muhammad (s) (*Muhammadī*). He never became angry, and we never heard him raise his voice while speaking. While he was gentle, he was also decisive and firm. He gave importance to praying on time, staying up during the nights of the month of Ramadhān, reading the Qur'ān out loud, and maintaining organization in all things. As a result of his strong, kind sentiment and extremely kind heart, he would never refuse anyone. One day he said to me, *"From morning until now I have answered the door 24 times in order to reply people's queries."*

'Allāma's daughter

Although he had very little time, 'Allāma managed his schedule in such a manner that he would spend one hour every afternoon with his family. During this time he was so kind and affectionate that one could not believe that this was an individual occupied with so much work.

'Allāma's daughter

At home 'Allāma was strongly opposed to anyone else carrying out his personal tasks for him. There was always a competition in turning down the bed [at home]. My father would try to carry out this task before anyone else, and my mother would try to anticipate him. Even in the end when he was sick and I used to go to his home, he would get up from his place to pour his own tea despite his state of illness. And if I objected and said, *"Why didn't you ask me to bring me some tea,"* He would reply, *"No, you are a guest, and you are also a descendant of the Prophet (s) (Sayyid), and I cannot give you any orders."*

At Home with his Wife

Ayatullah Ibrāhīm Amīnī

'Allāma's family life was extremely warm and pleasant. When his wife passed away he shed so many tears and was so saddened and moved that one day we asked him, *"We should be learning patience and endurance from you why are you affected such?"*

He replied:

Death is inevitable. Everyone must die. I am not crying for the death of my wife. My tears are for the kindness, housekeeping abilities, and the love my wife had. I have had a life full of ups and downs. In the holy city of Najaf when we were faced with many difficulties, I was not even aware of the needs and the administration of our life [because she took care of them so well]. Managing our life was in the hands of my wife, and throughout our life not once did my wife do something that I said *I wish she hadn't done that*, even just to myself. Nor did she ever not do something that I said *I wish she had carried that out*!

Throughout our life together never once did she say to me why did you carry out that particular act, or why didn't you do something! For example, you know that I work at home and am continually occupied with writing and studying. As a result I get tired and occasionally I need to rest and to renew my energy. My wife was aware of this. She would always have the kettle on and tea ready. Although she was busy with housework, she would pour me one cup of tea every hour. She would place it in my study and would return to her work until the following hour...how can I ever forget such love and kindness?!

'Allāma's daughter

His ['Allāma's] behavior with my mother was incredibly respectful and friendly. Through his actions it seemed as if he was always eager to see my mother. We never saw them order each other to do or not do anything, nor did we see any discord between the two of them. They were loving, loyal and forgiving to each other to such an extent that we thought they never disagreed.

The two of them were truly like two friends with each other.

Prior to her death, my mother was ill and confined to bed for 27 days. During this period my father did not leave her bedside for a single moment. He left all his work to take care of her.

At the same time my mother was an exceptional woman. She was patient when faced with difficulties and a meager lifestyle. She managed all our household affairs. She took care of our academic and social life and handled all our concerns. She worked with such efficiency and wisdom that my father was able to pursue his academic work with complete ease of mind.

Narrated by 'Allāma Tabātabā'ī

"It was this woman who allowed me to reach this position. She has been my partner and whatever books I have written, half [of the credit] belongs to her."

This one sentence from ʿAllāma Tabātabāʾī is sufficient as an indication of his enlightened view of women. At another time he said:

If a woman did not have importance, God would not have placed the lineage of the 12 Imāms in the progeny of Hazrat Zahra (a). Truly if a woman is noble and good she can make the entire world a rose-garden, and if she is bad she can make the world a hell... Women and men are partners, and after looking after the raising of her children, a woman must become aware and familiar with the affairs of her society.

At Home with his Children

'Allāma's daughter
'Allāma Tabātabā'ī was very affectionate with his children, as well as his grandchildren. Sometimes he would spend an hour of his valuable time listening to our chatting, or teaching us how to draw, or giving us exercises for our homework.

'Allāma's daughter
'Allāma valued his children, especially his daughters, a great deal. He considered daughters to be a blessing from God, and valuable precious gifts. He always encouraged his children to acquire the traits of honesty and tranquility, and liked that the sound and melody of the Qur'an should reach their ears. For this reason he used to read the Qur'an out loud. He gave importance to his children being well-mannered, and believed that the behavior of parents affects their children.

He was particularly respectful and loving towards his daughters, such that he would call them by adding the word 'sadāt' to their name, and he used to say that the respect of a daughter, especially a descendant of the Prophet (s) (*Sayyid*), must be preserved. He believed that daughters are a trust from God. However much a person pays them respect, God and the Prophet (s) are pleased [with him].

'Allāma's daughter

Our upbringing was not limited to our childhood. Even after I was married I used to always benefit from the guidance of my father. For example, in the early days of our marriage when I would visit my father's home, he would advise me by saying "Don't let it be the case that your actions result in the displeasure of Khānum (that is my mother-in-law), for God will not let that pass. You must make sure to assist her."

'Allāma's daughter

'Allāma had a close relationship with his children. In his final years when I was living in Tehran, I would visit him two or three times each week, but it wasn't determined exactly when I would go. Yet every time I would visit, his wife (his second wife) would say that it's been three or four hours that he has been pacing waiting for you. When I would ask how he knew I was coming, he wouldn't give me a clear response, and in the end I never understood how he was aware what time I would be arriving.

'Allāma's daughter

After the death of my son 'Hasan', he ['Allāma] came to Tehran. However, I didn't know how to behave with him so that he wouldn't become upset, and incidentally, he too, was thinking the same. When he arrived he asked, *"Najma, what can I say to you?"* I said, *"Nothing. All thanks belong to God"*. He replied *"All thanks belong to God, who, when he gave you a child, he gave you a good child."*

Sincerity and Humility

Ayatullah Ja'far Subhānī
Although we had a very close relationship with 'Allāma, not a single instance comes to mind of a situation in which he brought up a subject in the form of demonstrating [his knowledge] or that he presented some information without being asked a question.

Hujjat ul-Islam Mūsawī Hamadānī
Our teacher one day told me "I have never seen any one more ascetic than this man ('Allāma). Despite being a treasure of knowledge and information, he still stands to pray in the final row of Ayatullah Milānī's prayers amongst the travelers."

One of the Scholars of Qum
Once when one of the scholars of the religious seminary (*Hawze Ilmiye*) of Qum was praising the great Tafsīr al-Mizān in his presence, 'Allama said the following: *"Don't praise it lest I become pleased and my sincerity and good intention be destroyed."*

'Allāma Husayni Tehrānī
Every time I would meet 'Allāma, without exception I would try and bend to kiss his

hand and he would hide his hand under his cloak. He would display such humility and shyness that we would be startled. One day I said to him, "We try to kiss your hand in order to benefit from your blessed presence, why do you withhold this from us? Have you not heard of the hadīth of Imām 'Alī (a) that *'whosoever teaches me one word, he has made me his servant'*?"

He replied, "Yes, it is a well-known narration and its text is agreed upon."

I then said, "You are the one who has taught us so much and have thus caused us to be your servants over and over again. Is it not part of the etiquette of a servant that he kisses the hand of his master and thus receives blessings?"

With a charming smile 'Allāma said, "We are all the servants of God Almighty."

'Allāma Tehrānī

In the month of Sha'bān 1411 H, 'Allāma Tabātabā'ī visited Mashhad and came to our home. I gave him the library as his room so that he could use the books with ease. The time for Maghrib prayers arrived, and I spread a prayer mat for him and left the room so that he would start his prayers at which time I could return and pray behind him.

It was approximately fifteen minutes after Maghrib when he called for me. When I came near 'Allāma said, "We will follow you" [that is, I want you to lead the prayers].

I said "I request that you please go ahead and pray yourself!" [that you lead the prayers]!"

He said "We [I] have this request."

I replied "For forty years we have wanted to pray one set of prayers behind you, but it has not yet happened. Please accept."

With a charming smile he said "Then it is not much to add one year in addition to those forty years."

I said "I am your servant and your follower. If you order me I will carry out your order!" [to lead the prayers]

He said "I am not giving an order, this is just my request."

ʿAllāma Tehrānī

ʿAllāma Ṭabāṭabāʾī was a world of greatness. Like a regular seminary (*hawza*) student he would sit on the ground near the courtyard of the school, and when it was nearly sunset, he would enter Madrasa Fayziyya. When it was prayer time, he would pray in congregation behind the Late Ayatullah Āghā Hāj Sayyid Muhammad Taqī Khānsārī as if he was just another one of the students.

He was so humble and well-mannered and made such an effort to maintain his etiquette that I repeatedly told him that in comparison to your level of propriety (*adab*) and consideration we look ill-mannered!

Never once in almost forty years was he seen resting his back against a pillow. Rather, in front of guests he would always maintain his etiquette and sit a little distance in front of the wall. I was his student and often went to his house and in observance of etiquette, I wanted to sit slightly lower than him, but it was impossible. 'Allāma would rise and say "If that is the case, then I must sit either at the entrance or outside the room!"

Ayatullah Ibrāhīm Amīnī

I used to participate in the higher level (*darse khārij*)jurisprudence (*fiqh*) and principles of jurisprudence (*usūl*) classes of Hazrat Imām Khumaynī (qs) and the philosophy classes of 'Allāma Tabātabā'ī and was very attached to and loved both of these pious teachers very much. One day I invited both teachers to my room in Madrasa Hujjatiyya for lunch. They accepted my invitation and arrived at my room. I wanted to coerce the two teachers into a philosophical debate, but however much I tried I was not successful because they were completely free of any personal desire and thus avoided all types of academic argumentation.

In that session, if I addressed Imām Khumaynī and asked him something, he would reply and 'Allāma Tabātabā'ī would remain quiet and listen carefully. And if I asked 'Allāma a question, he would reply and Imām (r) would remain quiet and listen carefully.

Ayatullah Misbāh Yazdī

In the course of the thirty years in which I had the honor of being in his presence, never did I hear him use the word "I" on its own. On the other hand, I heard him use the expression "I don't know" many times in response to a question, the same expression that most people are reluctant to use. Yet, as a result of his extreme humbleness, this ocean of knowledge and wisdom used this expression with ease.

'Allāma Tabātabā'ī's son-in-law

One of the years when 'Allāma had traveled to Mashhad, we went to his house to visit him. Because of a weak heart and according to the orders of his doctor, he was strictly forbidden from sitting on the ground. As soon as we entered, he rose from his mattress and offered it to us to sit on. I refused to sit, and for some time both he and I were left standing until he said, *"Sit so that I can say something!"* I obeyed him out of politeness and sat. He too sat on the ground and then said, *"What I wanted to say is that it's softer over there."*

Ayatullah Jawādi Āmulī

I had written a paper on Imāmat and presented it to 'Allāma Tabātabā'ī, saying, "Occasionally when you are tired of studying and discussion, in the name of relaxation or as they say, for a recess (zange tafrīh) have a look at this paper of mine as well."

He kindly agreed and read the paper from beginning to end, word for word. After some time he said, *"I have seen it in its entirety."* When I went to pick it up from him, he made an objection saying that in a particular place in the paper you have made a personal prayer only for yourself. I had narrated a hadīth, and after the narration of the hadīth and a commentary on it, I had written *"O God, bequeath the ability to understand the signs of God to this being!"*

He ['Allāma] said, "Why have you made this personal prayer? Why have you not included others in your invocation for Divine sustenance?" Then he said to me, "As far as I am aware, I have never made a personal prayer only for myself."

Spirituality

Ayatullah Ibrāhīm Amīnī

'Allāma was in a constant state of remembrance of the Almighty (*dhikr*). When we would walk together, and our conversation would end, he would busy himself with *dhikr*. He believed strongly in supererogatory prayers (*nawāfil*) and sometimes he would even recite them while on the road. He gave great importance to participating in gatherings of mourning for the Ahlul-bayt (a) and shed many tears in grief for Abā Abdillah [Imām Husayn] (a).

He spent many nights awake and in worship, and in the month of Ramadhān, he would be awake, praying and busy with remembrance of the Almighty (*dhikr*) between sunset and dawn. He was the personification of the verse *Men whom neither merchandise nor selling diverts from the remembrance of Allah* (Sūra Nūr:38).

'Allāma's daughter

'Allāma Tabātabā'ī was not overly concerned with worldly matters. He used to say God is the one who gives reputation. Human beings can never attain status with worldly objects.

He had a very exalted and sensitive soul. Whenever God would be mentioned, his appearance would change. Occasionally he would tell me,"It is possible that sometimes a person becomes so unaware of God, that God inflicts him with a severe and dangerous fever for forty days so that he might once say from the depth of his heart *Ya Allah*, and fall into the remembrance of God."

In times of difficulty and pain he never displayed the smallest sign of distress. He confronted problems with serenity and patience.

Ayatullah Jawādī Āmulī

We were witness to the personification of asceticism (*zuhd*) in all the time that we spent with 'Allāma. Occasionally he would speak about the difficult years; the years when he was in Tabriz and his life was in turmoil. It was a time of unrest in Azerbaijan, but despite this situation and the fact that there was no outward peace for 'Allāma, he had no fear; such a situation did not shake him the least, and he remained firm [throughout].

Shahīd Mutahharī

In terms of spiritual perfection, 'Allāma Tabātabā'ī had reached such a level of *tajjarude barzakhi* that he was able to see visions from the world of the unseen which other regular individuals could not.

Years of spiritual exertion and endeavors on the path of self-purification and practical Gnosis (*'Irfāne 'Amalī*) resulted in [his complete] knowledge of theoretical Gnosis (*'Irfāne 'Ilmī*). That is because the late 'Allāma Tabātabā'ī united intellectual 'Irfān with practical 'Irfān, and thus was able to taste the reality of true 'Irfān. That which other mystics had written about in their books, he realized. He had in reality traversed the many stages of 'Irfān. In the end he wrote a timeless and lasting account of this. His book *Muhākemat bain Mukātebat* is a valuable text from whose valleys of knowledge many of those inclined towards 'Irfān have benefited from.

Allāma & the Qur'ān

Ayatullah Hasanzādeh Āmulī

'Allāma Tabātabā'ī was a live, moving manifestation of Sūra Al-'Asr from the Qur'ān. The reality of Sūra Al-'Asr had settled in him, and he had a special connection with this blessed chapter of the Qu'rān (*sūra*). In Tafsīr Al-Mīzan, he says about this sūra: "God Almighty has elucidated all the learnings of the Qur'ān and all the divine truths and truths about mankind in the small sūra."

'Allāma Tehrānī

'Allāma Tabātabā'ī was extremely humble and modest in relation to the Qur'ān. He would usually recite verses of the Qur'ān from memory and would tell us in which chapters (*sūwar*) those verses were located, and would also recite verses that were related to that particular verse. The sessions of Qur'ānic discussion of that late Sayyid ['Allāma] were extremely interesting and informative.

Hujjatul Islam Mūsawī Hamadānī

I remember once I had the Holy Qur'ān in my hand and a tafsīr in front of me. I wanted to open another book and at the same time I did not want the pages of the Qur'ān to close. As a result I placed the Qur'ān behind me on the ground. 'Allāma immediately picked up the Qur'ān and kissed it and then said to me, *"next time don't repeat this action."*

'Allāma's daughter

'Allāma would keep awake all the nights of the blessed month of Ramadhān, and he used to have a great desire to recite the Qur'ān and would try to recite it out loud.

Knowledge

Ayatullah Misbāh Yazdī

Classes of philosophy were looked down upon when 'Allāma first came to Qum, and much effort was put into closing his philosophy classes. However his gracious and wise manner and his kindly interactions with Ayatullah Al-Uzma Burūjredī won over some of his critics and decreased the influence of others.

'Allāma did not confine himself to the study of general philosophy. With the establishment of private sessions with prized students such as Shahīd Mutahharī, he began to study Western philosophies, in particular Dialectic Materialism. Together they ['Allāma and Shahīd Mutahharī] wrote one of the best books available in this field.

'Allāma's invaluable role in making the world aware about Islam, the teachings of Shi'ism, Islamic Philosophy and Gnosticism (*'Irfān*), and in presenting in writing the original ethos of Shi'sim, was a great and invaluable service that could only have been accomplished by such a man.

An indication of his valuable services is that it would be hard to find a single scholar in all of Iran and in many parts of the world [today] who has not taken from the harvest of knowledge and character of 'Allāma, and who has not directly or indirectly benefited from him.

Shahid Mutahharī

'Allāma Tabātabā'ī is an exemplar of men of worth and greatness. This man is so very remarkable and worthy that even after 100 years it will be necessary to sit and ponder and analyze his thoughts in order to fully understand his worth.

This man is truly among the most valuable servants of Islam. He is genuinely an embodiment of God-consciousness (*taqwa*) and spirituality. He has traversed exceptionally high levels of self-purification and *taqwa*. For many long years I have benefited from the blessed presence of this great individual.

To honor the likes of this great man is to honor knowledge itself, and to honor society... He is known as a distinguished intellectual, not only in the Islamic world but in the non-Islamic world as well.

'Allāma Sayyid Muhammad Husayn Tehrānī

One of 'Allāma Tabātabā'ī's students describes the way in which he met his teacher and began to study under him:

It was the year 1364 S (1985). I had moved to Qum in order to pursue my studies. I took up residence in Ayatullah Hujjat's school (Hujjatiyya), and was busy with my studies and discussions. The school building was very small and as a result the late Ayatullah Hujjat had bought the adjacent land in order to expand his school and build a new and spacious building; one that which, in accordance with the Islamic style of school, would take care of all the needs of its students.

Many engineers from Tehran and elsewhere came and presented various plans, but every one of them had some flaw and was rejected by Ayatullah Hujjat. This situation carried on for some time. Finally we heard that a Sayyid from Tabriz had come and drawn up a comprehensive and complete plan that was approved by Ayatullah Hujjat.

We were very curious to meet this Sayyid. Afterwards we heard that he had arrived in Qum from Tabriz, that he was known by 'Qāḍhi', that he was very knowledgeable in mathematics and philosophy, and that he had begun philosophy classes at the Hawza. We went to his house and realized that this celebrated and well-known man was the same Sayyid that we used to see walking everyday in the alleys. Never did we assume that he was an intellectual (let alone a scholar of many sciences). With a tiny burlap turban (emama) blue in color, without socks and with clothes simpler than average, he used to go back and forth in the alleys of Qum and live in an extremely small and simple home.

We were so enamored by 'Allāma Tabātabā'ī, and our desire to study with him so great, that we requested a private philosophy class with him. He magnanimously agreed and thereafter we were fortunate to be able to study both *hayāte qadīm* and Qur'ānic exegesis (*tafsīr*) with him.

Every day that passed our love for, and our relationship with 'Allāma, deepened, because he was a straightforward, noble, polite, and moral man free of any corruption. At the same time he was like a kind brother and compassionate friend to us. In the evenings when he would come to his room, in addition to the regular lesson, he would speak about the Qur'ān and knowledge of God Almighty.

Greatness and presence, tranquility and dignity, all manifested themselves in his existence. He was an ocean of knowledge that when penetrated, could provide the answer to every question. He would answer questions gently yet firmly, and with propriety and seriousness. Despite the fact that our debate and our impudence would occasionally reach high levels, never once did he raise his voice, always maintaining his patience and composure.

Ayatullah Jawādī Āmulī

'Allāma Tabātabā'ī's knowledge was so wide that he used to say:

"If the opportunity arose, I could explain all the issues of the Qur'ān from a single small sūra."

Ayatullah Jawādī Āmulī

In the year 1350 S (1970), we wanted to visit Makkah. It was winter, snowy and cold. We went to see 'Allāma Tabātabā'ī to convey our greetings and say our goodbyes. When our conversation came to an end, I said to him, *"Give us some advice that we can use during our travel, and that can be a provision for our journey!"*

He read this verse in which God says: Therefore remember Me, I will remember you (Sūra Baqara: 152). 'Allāma said

"Remember God so that God might remember you as well. When God remembers a human being, He delivers him from ignorance. When God the All-Powerful remembers a human being who is in the midst of some work, he will never find himself incapable of doing something. And if a human being were to have a moral problem, God, who possesses the Divine and Beautiful Names and is described by these great Names, would most definitely remember him, removing the difficulty and freeing him of that problem."

Ayatullah Jawādī Āmulī

'Allāma once told us that he visited the outskirts of Tehran one summer, where ideas of Communism and Materialism were prevalent. Some of those who held materialist views wanted to freely discuss their thoughts with him. He went to them and participated in a discussion from morning until evening, that may have lasted 8 hours.

He said, *"I discussed with this one individual using the view point of burhāne sidīdqiyīn (a Shi'ite philosophical proof of the existence of God)"*. Thereafter, this individual who was a Marxist saw one of his peers on a street in Tehran who asked him, *"Where did you reach in your visit and discussion with Agha Tabātabā'ī?"* He replied, "Agha Tabātabā'ī has made me a monotheist. He spent eight hours in discussion with us, and in the process he made one communist a believer in God and one Marxist a monotheist. He listened to every non-believer's insult yet never took offense and never quarreled."

'Allāma's daughter

Once 'Allāma Tabātabā'ī was informed that the Shah had decided to give him a PhD in philosophy. He became very upset and announced that under no circumstances would he accept such a thing. The head of the faculty of theology approached 'Allāma and insisted a great deal, but he continued to decline. In the end, after a great deal of persistence, the head of the faculty said, *"If you don't accept, the Shah will become angry and displeased...!"* 'Allāma responded explicitly, *"I have absolutely no fear of the Shah, and am not ready to accept this doctorate."*

Narrated by 'Allāma Tabātabā'ī

'Allāma Tabātabā'ī's Nastalīq and Shekaste handwriting [forms of Persian Calligraphy} were one of the best and most beautiful examples of calligraphy. Even though his hand was unsteady and his handwriting shaky towards the end of his life because of an illness of the nerves and tremors in his hand, the essence of the handwriting indicated that he was an expert in this art. He himself used to say, *"Samples of my handwriting remain from my youth and when I look at them I am amazed that this is my writing!"*

'Allāma Tabātabā'ī used to say:

Many days my brother and I would go to the outskirts of Tabriz near the foot of the mountain and the green hills, and spend the entire day from morning till dusk writing calligraphy... We used to spend all our money and time in buying paper and practicing calligraphy on it.

'Allāma Tehrānī

During the days when 'Allāma Tabātabā'ī was a learned scholar, a shining light, and a gathering place of knowledge and insight...in the days when he would walk the streets of Qum with clothes made of burlap, his outward appearance simpler than normal, staff in hand, going to and from the sacred shrine of Hazrat Ma'suma (a), the gaze of Orientalists and Western thinkers fell on the clear intensity of his thought and depth of his insight. His careful scrutiny, innovation, originality and resolute thought resulted in a growing suggestion in their minds.

The American government requested the Shah of Iran (Muhammad Reza Pahlavi) that 'Allāma be invited to teach Eastern philosophy in American universities!

In order to carry out this important request, Muhammad Reza sought help from Ayatullah al-Uzma Burujerdī – May God be pleased with him– informing him of the American request. Ayatullah Burujerdī in returned conveyed the Shah's message to 'Allāma. But 'Allāma's profound insight and sound judgment caused him to prefer a simple life, closeness with eminent scholars, a role in the spiritual atmosphere of Qum, and in training scholars in the hawza. As a result of all this, he rejected the request of the American government.

Allāma as a Student

Narrated by 'Allāma Tabātabā'ī

Allāma Tabātabā'ī narrates an account of the early days of his studies in the following manner:

In the early days of my studies, when I was occupied with studying Sarf and Nahw, I did not have a deep desire to continue my studies. As a result however much I studied I did not fully understand [the material]. I passed four years in this manner. Then one day Divine favor grabbed a hold of me and changed me and I felt a sense of infatuation and restlessness in relation to gaining knowledge, such that from that day onwards until my studies came to a completion approximately 18 years later, I never once felt tired or reluctant when it came to learning and thinking, and I completely forgot both the beauty and the unsightliness of the world.

I ended all dealings I had with those who were not part of the scholarly and academic tradition. I satisfied myself with the least possible amount of time for eating, sleeping and other necessities of life, and spent the rest of my time in my studies. It was very common, especially in spring and summer, for me to study from night until dawn. I would always study the following day's lesson from before. If a problem arose I would solve it even if it meant exerting myself to the utmost degree, so that when I would attend class I would be aware of what the teacher presented. I would never take an issue or a problem to the teacher.

Narrated by 'Allāma Tabātabā'ī

Allāma Tabātabā'ī describes his entrance into Najaf and the beginning of his studies in the following manner:

When I left Tabriz for Najaf with the intention of continuing my studies of Islamic sciences, I was unaware of the situation in Najaf. I didn't know where to go and what to do. On the way there I was in constant thought of what I should study and whose student I should become, and what path and route I should choose so that I might become the source of Divine pleasure and acceptance. When I reached the entrance of the holy city of Najaf, I turned towards the dome and

"O Alī! I have come in your presence so that I might continue my studies, but I do not know which path to take, and what program to choose. I want you to guide me to that in which there is goodness and moral soundness."

I [then] rented a place, and took up residence there. In those same first few days, before I had participated in any study sessions, I was sitting at home and thinking about the future when suddenly somebody knocked on the door. I opened the door, and saw that it was one of the prominent scholars. I greeted him, and he entered the house. He sat in the room and wished me well. His luminous face was striking and attractive. With complete pleasantness and sincerity he sat talking and I had a chance to get to know him better. During the conversation he recited poetry for me, and said something along the lines of:

"It is beneficial for someone who comes to Najaf with the intention of studying that in addition to increasing his intellect, he does not ignore self-purification."

After telling me this he left. In that session I had become enamored with his manners and his Islamic behavior. The precise and effective words of that saintly scholar left such an effect on my heart that I realized my plan for the future. During the time when I was in Najaf, I never left the presence of that pious scholar, participating in his classes of Akhlāq and benefiting from his company. That great intellectual was none other than Ayatullah Hāj Sayyid Mīrzā Alī Aghā Qādhī – may God be pleased with him.

Narrated by ʿAllāma Tabātabāʾī

(Narrated by ʿAllāma) ...One day I was standing in the madrasa when suddenly I felt a hand on my shoulder and heard this sentence:

"O son! If you want this world then pray the Night Prayer (*Namaze Shab/Salatul Layl*), and if you want the Hereafter then pray the Night Prayer."

These words had such a profound effect on me that from that day onwards until I moved to Iran five years later, I spent day and night in his presence. Not for a moment did I withhold from being in his blessed presence, and we kept in touch at all times until the end of his life. Throughout this time he used to give me prescribed instructions (*dastūrat*). He was none other than the late Ayatullah Hāj Sayyid Mīrzā Alī Aghā Qādhī Tabrīzī.

Friend of 'Allāma Tabātabā'ī

'Allāma Tabātabā'ī was so devoted to this teacher of his (Ayatullah Sayyid Qādhī) that when a friend offered him a bottle of perfume out of sincerity and affection, he replied:

"From the time of the death of the late Qādhī to this day, I haven't worn perfume and haven't felt like making myself sweet-smelling."

As a Student of Ayatullah Qādhī
Ayatullah Hasanzādeh Āmulī:

One of 'Allāma Tabātabā'ī's eminent teachers in Najaf was the great Ayatullah Hāj Sayyid Mīrzā Alī Aghā Qādhī Tabrizi, a Gnostic of great dignity, a jurist of elevated status, and one who enjoyed spiritual disclosures (*mukāshafāt*).

'Allāma Shaykh Aghābuzurg Tehrāni:

He, Sayyid Mīrzā Alī Aqā, was the son of Mīrzā Husayn Tabātabā'ī Tabrīzī Qādhī. He was a pious, moral, learned scholar and a jurist (*mujtahid*), whose friendship and acquaintance I had for tens of years. I saw him thus: That he had steadfastness and forbearance when it came to the path and method of akhlāq, and that his behavior was noble and magnanimous...

From among the memorable sayings of the late Qādhi is the following: "It is befitting if an individual spends half of his life searching for *insāne kāmil* (one of the special friends (*awlīyā*) of God)."

'Allāma Tabātabā'ī:

There are numerous accounts of the spiritual disclosures (*mukāshafāt*) of the late Qādhī. For example, he used to prepare the hearts of his students for accepting inspirations from the unseen (*ilhāmāte-ghayb*) by providing them with directives according to Islamic Law. He used to have a room in Masjide Kūfa and Masjide Sahla, where he would occasionally spend the night alone.

It is sufficient to narrate this one sentence from 'Allāma Tabātabā'ī, who was himself such a great scholar and commentator, about his teacher the late Qādhī, in order to understand Sayyid Qādhī's position:

"Whatever I may have, I received it from the late Qādhī, for it is either that which I learnt from him and gained from his presence, or it is that which I attained from this path which I also learnt from the late Qādhī."

As a Student of Ayatullah Qādhī

One of 'Allāma Tabātabā'ī's admirable characteristics was his acknowledgement of the efforts and work of men who contributed to the culture of pure Islām (Shī'ism), even if his own views were not in accordance with their views.

'Allāma often highly praised his late teacher Ayatullah Hāj Mīrzā Alī Qādhī Tabātabā'ī and repeatedly used to say *whatever we might have, it is from the late Qādhī.*

'Allāma Tabātabā'ī used to often mention the name of Bū Alī Sīna (Avicenna) and recognized him to be stronger in the art of intellectual proof *(burhān)* and philosophical reasoning *(istidlāl)* than Mulla Sadra, even though he greatly favored Mulla Sadra and his philosophical style and ability to change Greek philosophy, as well as his views of the doctrine of the fundamentality of existence *(asālatul wujūd)* and unity and gradation *(wahdat wa tashkīk)* in existence *(wujūd).*

'Allāma Tabātabā'ī was of the opinion that Mulla Sadra brought philosophy out from antiquity and breathed a new soul and spirit into the subject. As a result of this Mulla Sadra is known as the one who brought Islamic philosophy back to life. *(zindekunandeye falsafe)*

'Allāma Tabātabā'ī considered Bū 'Alī, Fārābī, Khāja Nasruddīn Tūsī, Bahmanyār, Ibn

Rushd, and Ibn Turke a few of the most outstanding and eminent philosophers.

Allāma as a Teacher

Ustād Rezā Ustādī

'Allāma Tabātabā'ī was one of those rare teachers who acquainted his students with the whisperings of life and the fountain of knowledge, but at the same time trained them with the light of love and self-purification...We have had and have many teachers; individuals who have many students. However every teacher does not guide and train his students. These are two categories separate from each other [ie. Teaching and guiding]. Some teachers teach for many years and concentrate only on imparting knowledge. 'Allāma Tabātabā'ī however, at the very same time that he taught his students, he brought them up as well, and day by day made them more accomplished.

'Allāma Tehrānī

What can I say about someone to whom I owe my life and my soul? From the time that God gifted him to us, he favored us with everything.

To us rash and rude students, he was gentle and tender. He was like a tall father who bends to take the hand of his child, and walks in step with him. He walked with and trained each of us according to our individual style, taste and varying aptitude. Even though divine secrets swelled in his luminous heart, he had a cheerful open and relaxed face, a silent tongue and gentle voice. He was always in a state of thought, and would occasionally have a tender smile on his lips.

'Allāma Tehrānī

Professor Corbin was an inquisitive French university student from the Sorbonne University of Paris. According to 'Allāma Tabātabā'ī he was a simple-hearted and just man who believed that among the religions of the world it was only Shī'ism that was a mobile and live sect. All other religious sects had completed their lifespan and no longer allowed for their followers to have expectation (*taraqqub*) and attain greater stages of perfection.

Professor Corbin's relationship with 'Allāma Tabātabā'ī began in the year 1968, and continued for 20 years. Corbin saw 'Allāma's precise vision and sharp-sightedness as potentially powerful and influential in the West and in Europe, and therefore carried out interviews with him. His goal was that the voice of Islām and Shī'ism should reach the ears of that part of the world so that they might too become aware of this knowledge that was intrinsic to the soul necessary for the growth of the soul. Eventually these interviews were published in four languages: Farsi, Arabic, French and English and compiled in a book by the name of Shi'a.

'Allāma's meetings with Corbin required a great deal of effort and struggle on his part, as he was forced to travel from Qum to Tehran by public bus so that he could talk about the truths of Shī'ism and introduce the true face of the concept of the possessor of the greatest sanctity *(wilāyat)* to him. But it quickly became clear that these efforts were in fact of great service to Shī'ism because Corbin recorded these meetings and made them available in Europe, spreading the truth of Shī'ism and even supporting and defending the religion through his own speeches and conferences.

Corbin was of the opinion that because Shī'ism believes in the existence of a living Imām, it is the only religious sect that it is still alive. This is because the belief and reliance on Hazrat Mahdī (a) will always remain established. The Jewish faith died with the death of Hazrat Mūsa (a), the Christian one with the ascension of Hazrat Isa (a). All other sects of Islām also came to a dead-end with the death of Hazrat Muhammad (s), whereas Shī'ism maintained that the authority, Imām and possessor of Wilāyat who is connected with the spiritual world and receives Divine guidance is alive, and therefore Shī'ism itself remained alive as a religion.

In this way Corbin himself was very close to Shī'ism and as a result of his interaction and discussions with 'Allāma Tabātabā'ī and his acquaintance with these truths, especially that of Hazrat Mahdī (a), an intense metamorphosis was apparent in him.

Eternal Manifestations

'Allāma Tabātabā'ī used to say "he (Corbin) frequently recites supplications from Sahīfāye Mehdiwiyye and cries as he does so."

Academic Activities

Ayatullah Ibrāhīm Amīnī

In addition to Qur'ānic exegesis (*tafsīr*) and philosophy 'Allāma Tabātabā'ī practically brought about Farsi writing into the hawza system. Before this time most publications were in Arabic and importance was not given in society to writing and publishing books in Farsi. However he emphasized that society was in need of reading material in these subjects, and that it was necessary that individuals take the effort to write and spread such material.

I remember that the fist article I wrote was with his help and guidance. Today many of those in the Hawza system who write and publish articles and books, are indebted both to Divine grace and 'Allāma's efforts.

Impact on the Hawza of Qum

In the year 1956 Materialist influence and propaganda were on the rise in Iran. The enemies had invaded the thinking and thought of the public, and no religious article or academic publication exited in Iran in answer to these doubts or that addressed the needs of the youth.

[In response] an organization made of elite members of the Hawza was formed. They approached 'Allāma and requested that he write an article in answer to the view of the Materialists. However 'Allāma rather than write the article himself, carried out an action that had a much more lasting effect. He put forward topics and requested members of the organization to prepare the articles. Two members of the organization, Shahīd Mutahharī and Shahīd Quddūsī were the ones who prepared a paper on the topic *The communal life of ants and birds.*

Imām Mūsā Sadr and a few others wrote a paper on *The Qur'ānic perspective on patience and perseverance* which was a topic under scrutiny by leftist groups. Sections of these articles were published, and in this manner 'Allāma also brought about the introduction of Farsi texts into the hawza.

Ayatullah Jawādī Āmulī

After the death of Ayatullah Al-Uzma Burūjerdī, 'Allāma Tabātabā'ī canceled a few of his philosophy classes and changed their topics to something new: discussions on an

Islamic government. 'Allāma even wrote a number of articles on this subject and circulated them among a group of jurists (*marāj'i*) and scholars, in which he emphasized that an Islamic government has great political power. One of the subjects that came up during that time and was also mentioned in his classes was the matter of Governance of the Jurist *(wilāyatul-faqīh)* and its relation to an Islamic government.

Ustād Ridhā Ustādī

'Allāma Tabātabā'ī spoke of an Islamic government after the period which followed the death of Ayatullah Burūjerdī because there was a vacuum and a conflict on this subject.

Throughout his intellectual life, 'Allāma Tabātabā'ī paid particular attention to addressing those matters which required attention. When Shahīd Mutahharī said "whatever academic work I carried out was in response to a need society had" – I am sure that this spirit and practice was taken from his teacher 'Allāma Tabātabā'ī.

Al-Mizan

Narrated by ʿAllāma Tabātabā'ī

When I cam to Qum, I studied the educational program at the Hawza, and I measured it with the needs of the Islamic society. I found deficiencies in it, and I felt it was my duty to try and eradicate them. The most important deficiencies in the Hawza program were in the area of Qur'anic exegesis (*tafsīr*) and intellectual sciences. As a result I began to study tafsīr and philosophy. Despite the fact that at the time tafsīr of the Qur'an, which is a science that requires research and scrutiny, was not being addressed, it was not considered worthy of study by those who had the ability to do research in the fields of jurisprudence (*fiqh*) and principles of jurisprudence (*usūl*). Rather teaching tafsīr was considered a sign of having weaker qualifications! However I knew I could not use this as an excuse in front of God [so as not to study tafsīr] and I continued my studies until I completed the writing of Tafsīr al-Mizān.

Narrated by ʿAllāma Tabātabā'ī

Initially I carried out an exhaustive research of Bihārul-Anwār in order that I might publish a work on a specific subject. Following that I put in a great deal of effort in gathering verses and traditions until it came to my mind that I should write a tafsīr. However I felt that the Qur'ān was an endless ocean and therefore I separated those verses relating to the hereafter and I wrote on seven subjects, until I came up with a tafsīr of the Qur'ān that was finally completed, comprising of 20 Arabic volumes. In this tafsīr, verses are explained using the Qur'ān itself as opposed to the views of the commentator. And I learned this style [of tafsīr] from my teacher the late Qādhī.

Shahīd Mutahharī

Tafsīr al-Mīzān is one of the best commentaries that has been written on the Holy Qur'an, and I can even claim that it is the very best commentary available among both the Shī'a and the Ahl-Sunna that has ever been written to this day.

Our people will only understand the worth of Tafsīr al-Mīzān after 60 100 years.

Ayatullah Hasanzādeh Āmulī

The best way to know what a great man he ('Allāma) was, is through his wayfaring towards God, and the intellectual effects of his teaching and writing. All the great individuals in the religious seminary (*hawza elmiyeh*) of Qum who have currently taken upon the task of teaching the principles of the Ja'farī school of thought were his students. His excellent Tafsīr Al-Mīzān that is the cause of pride in the intellectual world is one of his precious literary monuments and the mother of all his works.

Imām Mūsa Sadr narrated from Shaykh Muhammad Jawād Mughniye

From the time that I received Al-Mīzān, I no longer used the rest of my library, for this book was always on my studying table.

Ayatullah Hasanzādeh Āmulī

'Allāma stayed up on the night of Qadr researching and studying the verses of the Qur'ān and finally completed his tafsīr on this auspicious night, which is the equivalent of 1000 months. At last at the end of AlMīzān he wrote:

"With the praise and grace of God the writing of this book has come to an end on this blessed night, the 23rd night of the Holy month of Ramadhan..."

Ayatullah Makārim Shīrāzī

One day he ('Allāma) called for me and said, "I would like Al-Mīzān to be translated and I believe you should do this."

I accepted the offer and translated the first volume which was in Arabic – and contained very precise and condensed information – into two volumes [of Farsi]. One day I visited him and said, "Agha! You are a learned scholar but I am someone who cannot resort to others (taqlīd) in certain matters. Therefore as I translate your discussions do I have your permission to write any difference of opinion I might have in the footnotes?"

He replied with one meaningful sentence, "Let us discuss and criticize between ourselves first, and not among the public."

Accepting my point of view is an indication of his academic justice and noble spirit. From then on whenever I had an objection to make I would first discuss it with him, and if I was not satisfied then only would I write it in the footnotes.

'Allāma Sayyid Muhammad Husayn Tehrānī

One day I met 'Allāma Tabātabā'ī and said to him,

"This great tafsīr [Tafsīr Al-Mīzān] has not yet been recognized in the religious seminary (*hawza*) as it should be, nor have people realized its true value. Only if this tafsīr is taught in the hawza and discussed, and its contents critiqued and analyzed, then perhaps after a period of 200 years will its value be truly recognized."

Another time I said to him, "When I become occupied with studying this tafsīr, and when I see how you relate verses to each other and verify one with the other and thereby extract a meaning from them, I cannot explain it except to say that at that time divine inspiration must have taken over your hand."

He ('Allāma) shook his head and said, "This is just a positive outlook on your part, we haven't done anything!"

Perseverance and Hard Work

Ayatullah Ja'far Subhānī

'Allāma's nights like his days were spent in studying, researching and writing. Only on the day of Ashura [the 10th of Muharram] would he take a break.

He stayed away from useless discussions, futile night gatherings and fruitless visitations, and grieved deeply for lost time.

Sometimes when in the process of researching a topic he would lock himself in a room and not meet anyone unless it was necessary. He considered every moment in a man's life to be his capital. As a result when 'Allāma was in Tabriz, he was away from nearly everyone, and spent one season of the year in a village near Tabriz by the name of Shādgān. Preparations for Tafsīr al-Mīzān, reading once through Bihārul Anwār of the late Majlisī (r), and many other research projects in the subject of hadīth and other intellectual problems were carried out during this time.

'Allāma's daughter

Occasionally Aghā Quddūsī [Allāma Tabātabā'ī's son-in-law] and I would discuss the cause of [my father's] success, and the reason behind his progress. He would say, *"Aptitude is a very important factor in the progress of an individual. However perseverance also plays a very important role."*

'Allama had astounding perseverance. He spent many years working hard at his tafsīr, but he never got tired of it. [During this time] he wouldn't differentiate night from day. From early morning until noon he was occupied with researching and writing. Then after his prayers, a meal, and a short rest, he would once again busy himself with work and activity. This was despite the difficult conditions life dealt him the spiritual and mental blows one upon the other, the unremitting emotional bereavements, and the family tragedies and difficulties on top of all this. At five years of age his mother, and at nine his father both passed away, and the dust of grief of being an orphan settled deep into his spirit and soul ... [not to mention] the difficulties he faced in Najaf and in Tabriz...

Yet when a path is chosen and perseverance is there to help, a man's weighty duties become easy and simple.

'Allāma narrates:

When I was in Najaf I found a math teacher who was only free to teach at 1 in the afternoon. I would walk from one side of the city to the other side in the exhausting afternoons of Najaf. When I arrived at his location my clothes would be so drenched in sweat that I would enter the fountain [to shower], and after some time I would go near the teacher and study math.

Truly heat and cold, fatigue and distress had no meaning for him. This is because he took his work very seriously and had strong determination.

Spiritual Disclosures (Mukāshafāt)

Ayatullah Hasanzādeh Āmulī

'Allāma Tabātabā'ī said to me one day "Āghā every day that my attentive regard *(murāqabah)* is stronger, my ability to receive direct witnessing *(mushāhadah)* at night is clearer. Every day that my concentration *(tawajjuh)* is greater, my spiritual disclosures *(mukāshafāt)* at night are clearer."

Newspaper Jumhuriye Islāmi

After the tragedy of HaftumeTīr (the martyrdom of Ayatullah Beheshti and 72 top government officials), 'Allāma's friends and family did not want to inform him of the martyrdom of Ayatullah Beheshtī, on account of 'Allāma's illness. During this time one of 'Allāma's neighbors went to his room and 'Allāma said to him, *"Whether you tell me or you don't tell me about Aghā Beheshtī I see him in a state of heavenly ascension and flight."*

Narrated by ʿAllāma Tabātabāʾī

My wife and I were among the close family members of the late Mirzā Alī Aghā Qādhī. In order to maintain family ties and inquire about our situation, he would visit us at home in Najaf. We [the two of us] had repeatedly had children, but all them of died in their childhood. One day the late Qādhī came to our home at a time when my wife was expecting but I was unaware of this. When it came time for him to bid us farewell, he said to my wife, *"My cousin, this time this child of yours will live. The child is a boy, and no harm will reach him. His name is Abd ul-Bāqi."*

Upon hearing his words I became happy. God did grace us with a son, and unlike our previous children he survived and no harm reached him, and we did name him Abd ul-Bāqi."

Narrated by ʿAllāma Tabātabāʾī

From among the amazing and strange incidents is this, that there was a time when a letter written by my brother arrived from

Tabriz. In that letter the following was written:

One of my students was able to communicate with the soul of our father and we asked him questions and he replied. During the conversation our father said that he has a complaint about you because you did not include him in your intention and Divine reward (*thawāb*) of the tafsīr that your wrote.

No one was aware of this matter except God and I, and even our brother was unaware of this, as it was a matter related to an intention of the heart.

When my brother's letter arrived I was extremely ashamed. I said,

"O my Lord, if this tafsīr of ours has been accepted by you and has any reward, I give the reward as a gift to the soul of my father and my mother."

I had not yet written about this in reply to my brother's letter, when a few days later a letter arrived from him saying that this time when we spoke to father he was happy and said, "May God extend Sayyid Muhammad Husayn's life and aid him, as he has sent us a gift."

Narrated by ʿAllāma Tabātabāʾī

When I was studying in Najaf, I used to earn my living by receiving a monthly wage from Tabriz. Once, as a result of a conflict between the two countries [Iran and Iraq], my monthly salary was stopped and my savings were dwindling. One day I was sitting at the table studying when suddenly my train of thought was disrupted by the worry that until when will the strained relations between Iraq and Iran continue as we don't have any money, and we are strangers in this land. As soon as this though entered my mind I realized that someone was knocking loudly on the door. I went and opened the door and saw that there was a man at the door. He was tall, his beard was dyed with henna, his turban (*amāma*) was tied in a special manner on his head, and he was wearing a distinctive outfit. As soon as the door opened he said, *"Salāmun Alaykum"*. I replied his salām, and he said, "I am Shāh

Husayn Walī! God says [to you] "in these 18 years when have I ever let you go hungry that you have now abandoned your studies and fallen into the thought that until when will the relations between Iraq and Iran remained strained and when will they send us money!" Farewell to you!" I also bid him farewell and closed the door.

I sat at the table. At that time I lifted my head from my hands, and then a number of questions arose for me – that did I actually walk to the door, or did I witness this scholar sitting here with my head in my hands?! Had I been asleep or awake?! Had the man called himself Shaykh Husayn Walī or Shāh Husayn Walī. His appearance was not appropriate with the title Shāh, nor was I sure that he was a Shaykh!

Some time passed and these questions remained unanswered, until a letter arrived from Tabriz that I should go there.

In the morning, according to my regular schedule, I went to Najaf's Wādius Salām [graveyard] between dawn and sunrise, and walked between the graves reciting Sūra Fātiha. Suddenly I saw a grave that was obviously an important one. I read the gravestone and saw that after many inscriptions in praise of the deceased it was written: *the late Shāh Husayn Walī*! I realized that it was the same individual that had visited my home in Najaf. I looked at the date of his death and saw that it was nearly 300 years earlier.

I was surprised at his sentence *"In 18 years when have we ever let you go hungry."*, because I had spent 9 years in Najaf, and I was 35 years old. So why 18 years?! After some thought I understood that it was exactly 18 years that I had put on the turban (*amāma*) and the clothes of a soldier of Imām Zamān (aj)!"

Last Days

Ayatullah Ibrāhīm Amini

'Allāma Tabātabā'ī had completed the various levels of Gnosis (*'Irfān*) and wayfaring towards God and spiritual perfection. He was continuously occupied with remembrance of the Almighty (*dhikr*), supplication (*du'ā*), and intimate supplication (*munājāt*). When I would see him walking he would usually be reciting *dhikr* of Allah. When we were together during our sessions and the audience fell silent, it was apparent that his lips were moving with the *dhikr* of Allah.

During the last few months of his life, 'Allāma paid little attention to the matters of this world. He was unaware of worldly necessities and was wandering in another world. He had the remembrance of God on his tongue, and was removed from this world but attached to the next. In the last days of his life he even stopped paying attention to water and food. A few days before he passed away he informed one of his friends that "I no longer have any desire to drink tea and I have told them to light the tea kettle for me in the hereafter. Nor do I have any desire for food and I don't want to eat any more."

Afterwards he neither ate nor talked to anyone, but stared at the corner of the room with a look of astonishment.

Ayatullah Ibrāhīm Amīnī

During one of his last nights [before 'Allāma left this world] I was at his service. He was sitting in his bed, and staring at the corner of the room with penetrating eyes, but had no ability to speak. I wanted to hear some words and some instruction from him so that I might have a final memory of him, so I said, *"Do you have any advice for increasing one's concentration on God and presence of heart in prayer?"* He turned his attention towards me. His lips moved and with a barely audible whisper that could only be heard with difficulty, he said *"Attention in your relations with others (murāwadah), attention in attentive regard (murāqabah), attention in murāwadah"*. He repeated this sentence more than ten times. 'Allāma related this sentence at a time when he was unaware of worldly matters but had great attention towards spiritual matters and the remembrance of God. He considered prayers, attentive regard, controlling his soul and purifying it a way to increase presence of heart and continuous attention towards the Almighty.

One of the Scholars of Qum

During the last days of 'Allāma's life I used to go to his house in the afternoons to see if he needed anything, and to make him walk a little in his backyard. One day I said to him, *"Do you need anything?"* He said to me a number of times, *"I need...I need."*

I realized that perhaps 'Allāma's intention is something else, and that he was traveling on a different horizon. Then I entered the living room. 'Allāma also entered the room, and in a state whereby his eyes were continually closed, he became occupied with remembrance of the Almighty (*dhikr*). I wasn't able to distinguish which *dhikr* it was. The time of Maghrib arrived. I saw that 'Allāma, in that same state where his eyes were closed and without looking at the sky, became occupied with reciting the call to prayers (*adhān*) and afterwards he read his Maghrib prayers.

Days passed and his health worsened, and they moved 'Allāma to the Qum hospital. As he was leaving the house he said to his dear wife, *"I will no longer return."*

Ayatullah Ibrāhīm Amīnī

I was in Allama's presence on the last night before which they took 'Allāma to the hospital. For some time he was unconscious. After an hour he came to consciousness and sat on his bed for approximately 45 minutes. In the same state as he was in before, he stared at the corner of the room and then fell asleep. After some time when he became woke up he moved from his position as if he wanted to get up. We asked him do you want to get up? He said *"Those two individuals that I was waiting for have come."*, and stared at the corner dazzled and astonished.

www.ingramcontent.com/pod-product-compliance
Lightning Source LLC
Chambersburg PA
CBHW021450070526
44577CB00002B/342